WOMAN SURPRISED BY A YOUNG BOY

WOMAN SURPRISED BY A YOUNG BOY

Sheila Smith

Shoestring Press

Typeset by Nathanael Burgess
info@shoestring-press.com

Printed by imprintdigital
Upton Pyne, Exeter
www.imprintdigital.net

Published by Shoestring Press
19 Devonshire Avenue, Beeston, Nottingham, NG9 1BS
(0115) 925 1827
www.shoestringpress.co.uk

First published 2010
© Copyright: Sheila Smith
The moral right of the author has been asserted.
ISBN 978 1 907356 04 9

Front cover artwork: Woman Surprised by a Young Boy, 1991
© Copyright: Eileen Cooper. All Rights Reserved, DACS

ACKNOWLEDGEMENTS

Some of these poems have appeared in journals including *Agenda, Ambit, Iota, Stand* and *Staple.* Some have won awards, notably first prize in the Thomas Hardy Society's James Gibson Memorial Poetry Competition, 2008. 'At Renoir's House' was one of three poems chosen to be read by the author at the Kerry Arts Festival, 1998, and published in *Podium III, Poetry and Storytelling from Samhlaíocht Chiarraí,* Kerry Arts Festival, 1998.

I am grateful to John Lucas, Wayne Burrows, Michael Longley and James Greene for their help and encouragement, and to Eileen Cooper RA for permission to use her work as the cover of this collection. Also, thanks are owing to Nottingham women's poetry group, which I helped to found, for the pleasure and inspiration which our monthly discussions have given me.

Shoestring Press also gratefully acknowledges the work and assistance of Kimberly Redway.

For Nelly, and in memory of John

Contents

Haiku

in silvergilt sun
snow falls, apple blossom drifts
an erratic Spring

Kindred

Too late, by two hundred years,
to follow the zany path
of the Brown Satyr Butterfly.
No hope the Xerxes Blue will settle,
its home patch at the Golden Gate
wrecked by soldiers' boots and guns.
Another defeat for the Persian king.

But cheers for Californian Condors,
just hanging on, measuring thermals
wing-tip to wing-tip. An Ivory-Billed Woodpecker,
extinct, flew in the expert's face, reappeared
on America's east coast. No mate.
Ancient life sends out a ripple
before subsiding for ever.

Creation's leap-tide throws up new beings.
The Pill-bug's relative scrambles ashore
in California's Sierra Nevada, insides visible,
its long, bright, yellow liver. A tiny spider
fluorescent, brilliant orange. So new
they have no names, like creatures
in Alice's Looking-glass wood.

British farmers did for the Red-backed Shrike
or Butcher-bird, and the Short-haired Bumblebee.
But soldiers manoeuvring on Salisbury Plain
kick up the dust and encourage Devil's Bit Scabious,
food of the Marsh Fritillary, holding fast,
like the Wart-biter Bush Cricket in dwindling heath.
Stinking Hawk's Beard, gnawed by rabbits, vanishes.

Thugs, tough guys, thrive on urban sprawl,
desecration of moor, downs, woodland,
making others refugees or corpses.
The Augustan poet thought foxes in cities
an unimaginable sign of civilization's end.
Now they run scavenging London. Crows
make their nest in Farringdon Road.

Bully boy raven filches Snowy Plover's eggs,
slaughters Bank Swallows and Marbled Murelets.
Once sacred, symbolic, a creation deity,
now a pitiless executioner relentless,
hustling birds, tortoises to extinction.
Resting on power lines, it eyes windows.
Looks in a mirror. Sees a human face.

*With acknowledgement to Rebecca Solnit, citizen of San
Francisco, writer and naturalist, and Stephen Moss of the
BBC Natural History Unit, London.*

Death of a Painter

For Marjorie

In Provence rays of lavender
spread, deserted, in acrid perfume.
Fragile flowers on Greek islands
shudder in sun beneath olives
not seen by anyone. Nobody notices
how light sidles up the Eiffel Tower.

The roof of the well-worn minster
is high as a blizzard.
The coffin's shiny shell
low as mole-hills.
One sunflower, among docile blooms,
smoulders above you.

Those garden corners –
the weed surprised into bloom,
bold puckered ivy – will now never be looked at.
Lakeland fells, butting through shadows,
shift, and are gone, unrecorded.

'A Bone in my Leg'

The dead, expert in camouflage,
protect themselves, feeding us snippets.
A tilt of the head. A way of moving.

I recall my grandmother's face,
but could not draw it. I see
her feet grope in woollen slippers,

my dog, growling with jealousy,
snuffles after the nodding pompoms
across the mosaic rag rug.

We talked a lot, but I remember
one phrase only as I pestered her,
bouncing my ball, asking her to play,

'Not now, dear, I've a bone in my leg.'
'But so have I. That's all right.'
So many bones to creak and fail.

Shelter for them in her daughter's home.
Good walls, not her own.
Protection. They wrapped her round.

In her own way she escaped them
while ironing shirts, shelling peas.
And I escaped, and look back
to catch a whisper of her cologne.

Dementia

doors are where windows were

taking a stick to light the fire
my hand jars on the key in the lock

my comfortable house turns strange

how can I feel at ease in my house
where 'Open the door' means 'Shut the window'?

My comforting house grows cold

stooping to smooth the bed
I burn my thumb on the stove
'Yesterday I went away' is
'Tomorrow I return'

words whisk round corners
out of doors
sometimes – got it –
I pin it down
despite its wriggling
often it flips back
swimming away out of reach

the comfort of my house is gone

carpets crawl
along the wall
the electric switch
turns on the dark

the house stops spinning

familiar things glide into place
my hand and eye grasp them
words fall into order
one behind the other
docile passengers
in a well-regulated bus
knowing their destination

until the next time
thinking it the open window
I knock my head on the wall

Oasis

after a painting by Eileen Cooper

I love you
as amber weed
loves water-drift;
dependent
we float
unknowing
in love's sleep

over open sea
hungry birds
sail and dive
snatch flailing fish;
indifferent waves
lumber by
finger our rockpool

sea-fronds hold us
close;
small fish flicker, fade;
crabs dwindle to eyes
in fluttering sand

I am afraid
of the blue
open sea

Secret

In the early light, silent and cool,
they lurch and swing under my window,
their legs push up like pistons
surprising humps of brown and cream.

My bare knees hard on the sill,
leaning far out, savouring the danger
and the sweet strong smell of dung and mud,
I see a square head reach like a crane

and daintily snaffle a turnip for sale
in front of the village shop; it disappears
into the heave and toss of the hat-peg horns,
as the rope-end tails pitch round the corner.

To ride the tide

His soldier's boots rotted and stank
in foreign trenches for a Great War
which left a crater in his back,
dulled medals, bits from his Tommy's pack,
and jokes about old Fritz.

His policeman's boots in fourth position
hung about for 'early turn';
down creaking stairs in stockinged feet
out of the house to pound the beat –
a good job in the depressed Thirties.

His gardening boots dug a straight trench
ready to plant the Arran Banners;
the word he used was 'tilling' them
as though passing the time of day with Adam
over the allotment fence.

His bobby's boots took him through fire
sent from the sky (by Jerry now);
alerts, some 'purple', often 'red',
dragged him from his uneasy bed
to trawl the city's rubble.

His boots could stamp on more than toes
kicking aside precariously perched hopes,
scattering sandcastle schemes set in his way,
flattening them. Until his dying day
he'd beat time to a military band.

Shoes he never wore, except 'sand shoes'
yearly, for two weeks, by his Cornish sea.
Flesh cold, with lily legs, he taught me how to swim.
Tugged by the water's flow I held to him
thinking to ride the tide as easily.

Eclipse

His friend craned forward
to get into the picture.
But he, a true showman,
stood back, let the cameras roll,
held out his palm, shiny
with petrol or cooking oil:
the moon eating the sun,
darkening, chilling Tehran.

Elsewhere telescopes raised their snouts,
people jostled to peer into water,
or gestured with smoked glass
at a cloudy sky. But Omar,
aged ten, for two minutes
forty-five seconds held
the sun and moon
in his hand.

Cherry

"He was a man who used to notice such things." Thomas Hardy

At the end of winter's tunnel
uncertain flickering light.
Could be a trick of the pallid sun.

Another day or two and, unmistakable,
the cherry's fireflies gathering at last,
a fluttering swarm, homing in

thicker, faster. They become a storm,
pale fire igniting the yew's dark,
making livid the indigo sky.

Too high to thrust a hand
into the foam, not white, not rose,
cascading. The scent half-imagined.

Tossing beckoning arms
put out more flags, more frills,
defying gale, downpour, pigeons.

Turn more sedate as the days grow,
drop confetti for leaves translucent
as watered wine, prepare
for the seriousness of fruit.

Solution

You don't expect, when you open the door,
on entering the room, a clustering of wasps
nosing and hovering outside the window,
supplicating the corner of the garden wall.

On entering the room. A clustering of wasps.
Some hung treading the air, contemplating,
supplicating the corner of the garden wall
inquisitively, then lurched skyward.

Some hung treading the air. Contemplating.
They socialised. They grouped together
inquisitively. Then lurched skyward.
The inviting space blurred with them.

They socialised. They grouped together.
The work required a massive number.
The inviting space blurred with them.
Suspended. Protected by the wall.

The work required a massive number.
Specialists, workers, to build a nest
suspended. Protected by the wall.
Dreaming a paper palace with domes.

Specialists, workers, to build a nest
delicate, strong, fit for queens.
Dreaming, a paper palace with domes.
A storm of rain did not deter them.

Delicate, strong, fit for queens.
Intent on architecture of the grand kind.
A storm of rain did not deter them.
In fright I summoned a white knight.

Intent on architecture of the grand kind
they reckoned him of no account,
but in fright I summoned a white knight
protected by a veiled Renaissance hat.

They reckoned him of no account.
But his deadly powder gave him power.
Protected by a veiled Renaissance hat
he choked the swarm and poisoned it.

His deadly powder gave him power.
The paper palace remained a dream.
He choked the swarm and poisoned it.
Just one or two remained to mourn.

The paper palace remained a dream.
I should have liked to see it built.
Just one or two remained to mourn.
They are dangerous. Their sting can kill.

But I should have liked to see it built,
how the chewed bits became a realm.
But they are dangerous. Their sting can kill.
I had to move quickly to get them gone.

How the chewed bits could become a realm…
watching them gather and work together.
But I had to move quickly to get them gone.
Now there's no movement on the wall.

Watching them gather and work together…
nosing and hovering outside the window.
Now there's no movement on the wall
you don't expect when you open the door.

Home

In front, a table-cloth of grass,
a lavender hedge, bees in its bonnet.
The coat-dark, bike-blocked passage
to the garden: tangle of raspberries,
giddy towering daises, a wall
white-washed each Spring.
My hand remembers my dog's tough fur
as we sat on the path, and I smell
the kitchen cloudy with lentil soup
or warm with billowing saffron cake
and, on Mondays, the sick-wet stench
of clothes seething fast in the copper.

A narrow bedroom, my kingdom.
My pride, a dwarf pot of fake flowers
stuck to the most beautiful picture
I'd seen, a girl looking up through
branches and blossoms.

No matter that now
someone has ripped out the lavender,
built a breezeblock fence.
Like a turtle, I take what it was
always with me. You can move houses.

Instant Extension

To-night the wind-choir performs again,
seamless unison. Never a wrong note
from fine-tuned violins, contralto cellos,
perfectly blended through high trees.

Too close for comfort. I go
to draw long sheltering curtains
and stare, not through the looking glass,
yet into a fantasy garden.

Jasmine strands signal distress
among pictures, frames double-rimmed.
In agitated bushes the lamp
shines clear and still. Twigs scrape books.

Over the table clematis rampages.
Camellias pound the carpet. Stifling
the door, a honey-suckle trellis.
A woman is looking in, anxious.

Visit

Agitated behind the crinkled glass
you paddle to negotiate the door,
steering your wheelchair like a skiff.
Butts, precise in the ash-tray,
peg out a wilderness of unwanted time.
Moulding your dangling hand to its head
the stray cat leans, stiff with anticipation.
Once we swapped tales of love and conquest;
now news feels like exchange of prisoners.
The hands of my watch petrify.

Yet a name, a title of a film, a book,
sets your frozen language flowing,
returns your face handsomely to life
as a cinema projectionist
awakens glamour on an empty wall.
Vacuity seeps back like a stain.
Leave-taking seems escape,
past the mop-head of useless coats.
Trying not to flee, I pause on the step,
admire the scentless roses,
and, as the door snaps shut, turn
to stare myself in the face.

Silence can be very loud

The rare white-starred magnolia,
flourishing against the odds,
is no compensation for your not
being here to admire it;
nor the gleaming new studio,
conjured from the Victorian outhouse,
which you never used.

Silence can be very loud.

The exuberant snowy tree
in the driveway, celebrating Spring,
sings an obtrusive song.
White, for the Chinese, signs death.

The studio door's clear glass
takes the eye. Above, dull red
pantiles, fluted pie-crusts,
angled to catch the sun
hidden in grey Midlands cloud.
In front, the gravel terrace,
an iron table and two chairs.
Two glasses sing sapphire,
waiting for someone. Inside,
smell of new paint, rich wood.
Canvases give Mediterranean light,
busy with boats, fishermen,
whitewashed houses, hot sand, camels.
A poster of the last exhibition.

I cannot imagine you working
in that elegant, perfect place.
You were movement and laughter,
risk at the edge of both.
You drew your pictures from men,
marching, working women,
coalmines derelict, overgrown.

But at the back of your house,
in your old workroom, you're there.
Green light flows from the orchard,
mysterious with shadows and moving birds.
Your tumbled notebooks
in loved disorder scribbled
with flowers, shops, lakes,
wind worrying washed clothes, nets hung,
mended, dry, fells rearing out of mist.
Piled books, Turner, Klee, Constable,
Hockney, constant conversation
and argument with well-tried friends.
Brushes bristle out of pots like plants.
All colours that sang to you on the palette.
Stacked canvases along the wall.

Always risk at the edge of your laughter.
This room rings with it.

Burial

The shiny brass and varnished wood,
which has nothing to do with you,
yet haunted me as a revenant would,
the shiny brass and varnished wood,
in the black rain as lonely I stood
to board the train, taking me to
the shiny brass and varnished wood
which has nothing to do with you.

Mourners trailed over the graveyard grass,
wet, and crushed from last night's gale.
I let the family and coffin pass as
mourners trailed over the graveyard grass.
Sun lit a gate where a roan horse was,
a robin's song fell shrill and frail.
Mourners trailed over the graveyard grass,
wet, and crushed from last night's gale.

As though my heart had found its king,
and lodged where it had always been,
when I stood at the earth's black opening
as though my heart had found its king
my flowers flew like a bird's wing
to your breast. The throw quick and keen,
as though my heart had found its king
and lodged where it had always been.

'I've lost My Boat, You shan't have Your Hoop'

The white dog stands
reflected in wet sand,
turns to his master, running
with fishing gear to low tide.
The black dog leaps in front
his dark self at his heels.
Dangling smudged overhead
the new moon ('putty'
to *The Times* reviewer)
lays a path, silver-gilt,
through dwindling waves,
calm enough for paddlers.
A steamer balanced on
the horizon's tight-rope
adds grey to the sky's dusk.
'I've lost My Boat,
You shan't have Your Hoop'
shouts the over-dressed boy
to his over-dressed sister,
both struggling against
their mother in satin and bonnet.
Their shoes will be ruined.

All paint. On cracking canvas.
And Turner's ageing eye and hand.
That cross-wave travelling westward
will break before we turn away.

J.M.W. Turner (1775-1851): *The New Moon; or, 'I've lost My Boat, You shan't have Your Hoop'* exhibited the Royal Academy, 1840

Excavating the Takla Makan, the edge of China

Our treasure is neither silver nor gold...

The desert rang down sand curtains
but frayed fingers poked through,
surfacing, after millennia, like murder.

...our treasure is neither gold nor silver...

Quiet violence cradles a woman
laid, dusty, bristling plaits still yellow;
beauty's serene indifference

...our treasure is neither silver nor gold
but spry little horses with racketing hooves...

beauty unmoved by the snotty child
thrust screaming – still screaming –
under the earth; an improbable guide;

...our spry little horses with gusting manes
carry us up to the sweet high pastures...

improbable guide to paradise, promised
by the high-hatted high-priestess watching,
eyeless, behind her fence of teeth.

…the cloudy pastures feed our sheep
shaggy with wool we weave and dye
red, blue, green – enduring rainbows
found scarfing crushed leathery faces
polished by the industrious sand;
cardboard hands; scarecrow noses.

Our treasure is neither gold nor silver
but: spry little horses; slub and twist
of scarlet cloth; an oval face
seen now bobbing between market stalls
or drifting at the tail of the tilting cart
set on towards the west.

At Renoir's House

A green bowl
on a green plate;
in grained wood
a jade eye, open.

Giving the room its room
I stand aside,
left; alone for me floats
the plate, the bowl,

shifting green like light
through water over sand;
solitary, taking
the table's centre,

on a sheen of use
and years; bentwood
chairs put two
and two together.

From the white dresser,
against white panels,
a matronly jug
returns the green message.

The Alice looking-glass
plays a hand of family snaps,
re-invents the jug.
His paintings crane forward.

Upstairs, his long brush,
clamped in his hand's
arthritic claw, coloured
porcelain summer Sundays.

Sometimes he turned
at the stir of the orange
and olive trees; peered for sails
clipping the sea.

Petticoat curtains swing
on the herringbone floor;
the half-shuttered sun
ripples round bowl and plate.

Clay, drawn true by
the potter's thumb.
Resting. On wood. Waiting for
children. Visitors. Still life.

Two for Lunch

Gull mobiles turn
above the station road.
It runs full tilt to your door.

Rows of artisan houses –
yours untouched, original –
where railwaymen lived.

Through downstairs windows
harvest of books, each sheathed
in brown paper, title precisely inked.

Notices against the glass:
socialist meetings, exhibitions,
charred by time. The bell is silent.

But you appear, arms wide
like a welcome chair.
'It doesn't work in wet weather.'

I follow your emerald shirt
up, up the clattering stair
to your seasoned table. Salmon,

wine you're not supposed to drink.
It could be a love-feast,
presided over by paintings, pots,

glass, prints. Gifts from so many friends.
Hand-milled paper you like to touch.
You know so much, so much,

where Turner travelled,
how Morris learnt to print.
Ford Madox Brown's murals, canvases.

Rage against Roger Fry,
'That old cawing crow'
deserting English painters

making fashionable the French.
Head on hand, you quote Dickens,
Barnes. A Victorian sage at ease.

I drift into the picture, losing time,
trying to fix it sharp, clear,
knowing the colours will run.

Strong shoulders still; bear hug,
though I can't get close.
You keep your secrets well.

Eye to eye with a patrician gull
you tow your years, a sturdy tug,
knowing this shifting coast.

Transfiguration

Bach's St Matthew Passion in Amsterdam

Unhurried, trickling down scarlet stairs,
blossoming, a black and silver rose,
the banked choir and orchestra
confront us like interrogation.

St Matthew's gospel, some say,
was dictated by an angel, pictured
confiding. Or Caravaggio's holy astronaut,
over the saint with writer's block.

In the storm's eye, a double bass
played by a towering man,
his baroque bow delivering arrows
to pierce the chandeliers.

The cavernous hall, electric with listeners
to the barrage of voices. Hushed to a lull
shattered. My God, my God, why
hast thou forsaken me?

Challenge louder than thunder,
more comprehensible than the final
triumphant notes pounding
the ornate ceiling, supporting Paradise.

We shout with approval. No question.
In the historic hall, in the city
scattered with monuments to the war
dead, imprisoned, tortured. Become a crowd.

People talk to each other, compare
news of this notable death. The angel
has departed. The big musician left,
standing, ordinary, in a creased suit.

Without Surprise

Behind that door, in that back street,
Prague again plays host to Mozart,
jokey as usual, in frock coat and wig,
conducting *Don Giovanni*.
Sometimes, dangling above the players,
big thumbs and fingers hover,
dwarf the Don on stage
lusting in spasms.

Convulsed by his own genius,
Mozart bends this side and that,
graciously acknowledges the audience,
jerks his frisky baton,

arouses the Commendatore's bass,
the vengeful statue accepting the Don's
sardonic invite to supper –
'Si! Si! Si!'

The miniature world shatters.
A giant arm, daubed with plaster,
whisks away the defiant Don –
Heaven? 'No! No! No!'

Outside the moon prepares
her own stage set. Empty. Limelight
exposing deserted streets,
shadowing doorways.

Inside, monstrous hands hang up
sagging puppets one by one.
They sway. A dismal row.
A mass execution.

To wade through the moon-flood
through Chirico perspectives
        fooled by cul-de-sacs
is to look for Hell's mouth
        at each doorstep
without surprise.

Shadow and Sun

Yellow gault bricks, clay and sand
but enduring, drink the sun in
Corpus Christi Old Court
pampered with grass
long since forbidden to those
not Fellows. A rule unknown
to pious scholars who filed
through the sagging arch
to sing masses for anxious souls
in St. Bene't's, of the Saxon tower.
"The oldest college gateway
in Cambridge." A trestle,
white linen, college glasses
shooting rainbows, on the lawn
where children run, or jump
trodden, shadowed stones
edged black as funeral stationery.
Flutter of summer dresses,
of greetings concealing the shock
that friends age. A Golden Wedding.

Lunch over, we walk straggling
along the hot path over the river.
Minnows crowd under the willows,
send tiny replicas over the sand,
pause, move, all one way,
synchronised swimming,
satisfying, living pattern,
suddenly obliterated. A boy
leans to catch them in his hat.

Shadowed, a large fish hangs
unfazed, idly sways.
Everyday, friendly grass in
our hosts' garden where
anyone can sit, forgetting
time under benign trees
half believing it can be stopped.
Right, in a way. This sun and shade
will be replayed many times.
For consolation.

In Pembroke Chapel

Madder and indigo, onion-skin gold
and murex purple, substantial cushions
in voluptuous wool, each one different.
If you sit in the topmost tier of the stalls
your service paper rests on one.

They are the gift of Matthew, Bishop of Ely,
proud of his clever nephew, Christopher Wren,
the Chapel his first completed building.
The old Bishop funded it, thankful
to escape the Tower: eighteen years for the wrong faith.

Also he knew the Fenland chill
in the bones, and how a cushion
is a godsend, makes all the difference.
Now there was a king on the throne,
the Church Established, the Chapel built.

Victorians disturbed its perfect proportions.
Two leprous pillars menace the altar
but fail to extinguish Wren's honey-gold wood,
plain pillars at the Chapel's entrance.
In the ante-Chapel the tiny alabaster Virgin,

with a well-flung cast of her rosary
(each little bead perfect) tips St. Michael's scales
in favour of a terrified soul, defeats the Devil
crouched waiting in a corner. Comforted,
I pat my cushion. Some love tokens endure.

Only Fellows may walk on the grass...

and the tall moustachioed man
in licorice black boots. A toy soldier
from an old-fashioned nursery.
A subsidiary forester in *Der Freischutz*.
A left-over officer of the Austrian Empire.
He trundles a little plastic watering tank.
His crisp gentian shirt and black cap
bisect the ragged fingers trailed by birches,
not yet in leaf, bordering the path.
Reaching the green's further edge
his ramrod back swivels. He stops.
One step back. Position the machine.
One step forward. Push.
From the tank's blunt nose
two little fountains sparkle over the grass.

Blue House

Just a dark house on the road
a point to make for, then turn back
savouring the unaccustomed warmth,
pausing to lean upon that bolted gate. Then goad
our feet a few more yards uphill
to bring in view the muttering watermill.

But on that cloudless night the full moon
aimed its shaft of light across the Aegean
directly to the villa's hidden back.
We saw the windows at the front become
tall blocks of ebony in a wall of indigo.
The house was blue with secrets. Stars hung low.

Away from that land of goddesses and heroes
the blue house still lingers in the wings,
waiting to command the mind's flickering screen,
that mad eternal cinema where anything goes.
Sometimes a hovering, half-blurred image.
Or a full dress performance, centre stage.

In dreams I push the gate ajar, approach the door.
It shifts an inch. Inside, a hand or foot against it?
At once I'm in the garden. At the back.
No moon. Black as anthracite. Lower
than the road. Concealed. I grope at air,
calling my friend. No one is there.

Only early risers

                    are privileged
to see the great northern diver
take his bath, lift his wings
clear of Shetland water,
the tumbling bay by the Ness
in the peaty-green island Yell.

Mary's white, small house on the shore,
The Booth, once a fisherman's home,
crouches below the moor's slope
where trolls leave their tracks,
and the stove, the settle, the chairs, the beds,
dragged from the road at the top, left theirs.

The crofter built her a peat pile
like an upturned boat, left spaces
for wind to nuzzle through and dry;
stranded heather roots, hooks and knots,
give burning turf its honey tang.
From the stack, light and clean to collect.

I lean in the early morning cold
at the door where once the fisherman's kids
ran home. Porridge gasps on the stove.
I wait for Mary, dipping her seventy years
in the chopping, chattering sea,
the great northern diver gone.

North Sea Turbulence

Shetland sent me wild for the fiddle,
for trolls, seamen, great lumps of water,
desperate to hear the Forty Fiddlers,
unsmiling men who, as one, swept the sea
from their chests, kept pace with gales.
Jimsie, lithe and spry as a robin,
wielded the peat spade like a scalpel,
took off slices clean as bricks,
built boat-shaped stacks holed
for the north-easter to blow through,
drying heather roots for winter fires.
Lollie's hand, big as a leg of lamb,
coaxed his boat through the surge
off Sumburgh Head; Tom slipped brown wool
from a morrit sheep neat as a baby's coat,
whipped his fiddlestick with a flick
to send every foot tapping, like Aly,
lured by the fairies to play
for three centuries at their ball.
Johnny navigated 'blowing smoke'
to Foula, Isle of Fowls and headlong cliffs,
knew the right tide to visit
the beckoning Caves of Papa Stour.

Defying their dark Sunday suits and ties,
the great bank of Fiddlers as one,
plying fiddlesticks. Their harmonised roar.
That night they stood proud on the platform
in full command of their ship.
Should it up anchor I didn't care,
if, fiddles flying, it took me into the dark,
threaded the islands, skirted the Out Skerries,
till it shook the echoes from Fingal's Cave
or the grass-grown street of St Kilda.

Windhoose, Isle of Yell

Smallish windows are set
in calloused stone, four-square,
to look away from the sea,
the storm's clatter. But now,
with one wall down, the eyes
look straight through, lidless,
commanding rocks surfacing,
boats nuzzling shore, clouds.
And, this way, sheer turf slope,
stained with three bruises.
Workmen building, digging,
once unearthed a skeleton,
brittle, angular, splayed
under the threshold block.
If murder, it was long ago.
But those three marks, maps
of hell, giants' tears.
They never fade, even in Spring.
At sunset they burn copper.

I never go nearer than this.
Mary prised tiles from the ruin,
set them beside her muttering stove.
The booth door open, they shine,
jewels, wet shells, witches' teeth.
I'd not step over the door stone
for fear of the tale of the sailor,
wrecked by the hungry rocks,
bivouacking there for days
and the holy nights of Christmas.

Then cloud put out the stars.
He opened the door, hard against
horror. The cloud sank down, down.
From the porch he threw up an axe,
and again, and again, running
down the frost-steeled turf.
Sagging gouts of blood fell,
troll's blood, one, two, three
on the turf, where they burn now.

After, the house was at peace.
But I never go nearer than this.

To Camera: Roads

1

No other place to sit
except the road, quiet
since the lorries left
with men, tied like calves.

What matter? The woman
has no neighbours now.
Her house cracked open,
spilt from its walls.

On stones and dirt she sits,
in her good coat, salvaged.
One hand shields her face
from her neat little daughter.

Solicitous, the child leans
with reasoning concern,
spreading hands too small
to hold a crumb of comfort.

2

Smirking and stamping, dragons,
on Beijing's busy road.
Unused to city dust and celebration,
father sits marooned with son.

Big blue hands, now idle,
above a bowl empty of offerings;
he squats, a distraught god,
a Mongol emperor, defeated.

His miniature self, his son,
twisting against bundled clothes,
half-blinded by his knitted hat,
the village pattern, red and black,

offers a biscuit. He knows
hunters must have food
to get their prey. Here, just one.
Before they're gone.

Woman Surprised by a Young Boy

after a painting by Eileen Cooper

She had one child,
she wanted no more,
but her husband did.
She walked on the shore;

by the furtive waves
she walked and sighed;
then home through the moor
as daylight died.

The heather cocked a bloodshot eye
watching her on the road alone.
She skirted the hill and
met her son.

His arms spread in welcome,
greeting his mother;
he held out his second head
to start his brother.

Away on the hill
his brother to be
capered and sang
with relentless joy.

She froze on the road,
knew the tender snare:
night, hill, the child
trapped her there.

Road, moor and sky
were open and wide;
she knew the old prison of love;
she walked inside.

Music

She wore red. Red lipstick,
smudged. Her hair short,
spiky as though rising
with joy at music. A pianist.
Direct, to an unseen listener,
she talked of Theresienstadt
where the Nazis herded Jews.
'White water at breakfast.
Black water for dinner,
for supper. We were starved.
We made music in bitter cold,
and we were happy, healthy.'
But so many died. Efficient SS
crammed the final transports
east, where the sun rises also.
The lost composers and musicians.
'At first we didn't know about
Auschwitz. Later we knew.
They began to build gas-chambers
at Theresienstadt but ran out of time.'
Her face round as a ripe apple.
Her eyes sharp as starlight.
'If you have music you are happy.'
She is ninety-eight. 'It is the music.'

Hot and Cold

Nelly, with scholarly concentration,
examines the café's 'carte',
and, smiling, finds 'Rhum grog'.
She says it kept her warm

those winter days she stopped
at all the cafés, though late
for lectures at the Sorbonne.
Running to make up lost years

when cold, more lethal
than the Seine's savage chill,
and the hurry to exhaustion
were the way to death.

Then she dreamt paradise –
a hot potato. Hunger fades. Ice burns.
Even in hottest summer she carries
flame marks of ancient deadly frost.

Down near the Pont-Neuf, in pallid sun,
hovering above funereal traffic,
an angel, newly bright in sugary gold,
offers the unforgiving dead a laurel wreath.

Prague's Old Jewish Cemetery

Death is deep, green, stony.

No burials here for centuries,
but headstones crowd, importunate,
eager to put their case.
Some bow, thankful to survive.
Some lean back against time, weary.
Others proffer little cairns,
each pebble hard as tears.
Fearful I might dislodge them,
disturb the ancient dead,
I edge along erratic paths,
bend, peer from a distance
at inscriptions. Symbols.
Carp swim in stone, and other creatures
stag, fox, lion, bear – family names.
'In those days', the keeper tells me,
'there was a massacre of the Jews.'

I feel crowded, chilled,
look behind me, frightened
to glimpse the Golem, created
by Rabbi Löw to be his
giant, servile, serving-man.
Though slain for rebellion
surely he plods here still
on his shadowy errands
in this city of magic,
in this plantation of grave stones.
Some grimed with ashy stains
as though flames had reached this far.

In the Holocaust Memorial Garden, Beth Shalom

roses called white
are mostly cream
luxurious

but these are
luminous throwing
light on their half-acre

all the same height
none above the others
each with a plaque at the foot

clumps of sturdy stems
rooted strong in the compost
the compliant earth

exchanged for desolation
disaster loss of those
whose names shine near the soil

people stoop to read them
it takes time there are so many
footsteps accentuate the silence

the fragrance sweet
but faint as joy
and family long past